Janet

Dancing in the Rain

Your presence makes a difference in the world

Marcia A. Williams

Enjoy the journey

Marcia

To order additional copies of this book, contact:
Xlibris Corporation
1-888-795-4274
www.Xlibris.com
Orders@Xlibris.com
67458

Acknowledgements

To my family and friends: Thanks for your continued support of my goals and dreams. I am eternally grateful.

Thank you Gordon and Benjamin for giving me a reason to smile everyday.

Cover Image: Marcia A. Williams
Cover Design: Jerry Ples

Introduction

Dancing In The Rain is a celebration of life's lessons of love, empowering us to go out into the elements, torrent or tepid, open our arms to the sky while splashing into puddles with enthusiastic joy. Yes, life and relationship brings heartache but as long as there is pulse, the eternal beat of love that drives us towards purposeful living, all is well with the world. In family, friends and faith we find the tools to construct our temples of happiness that offer solitude, silence and a safe haven to encounter peace. Dancing In The Rain is a totem of guiding faith that becomes an essential aspect of our journey to fulfillment.

We all know a Daughter of the King. She is our best friend, our sister, our lover; one who stands for all that is good and real in our lives. She loves fearlessly, willing to taste suffering if only to share with us the path of least resistance. She is adored by many for the grace and charm she exudes effortlessly. And yet she feels, deep and bold, questioning the very experience she champions only to emerge more than woman.

The stages of relationship, loss, suffering, healing, rebirth, resolution are presented here in poem and prose. Anger, Silence, Solitude and Loneliness are universal in appeal. Words are regal too when spoken by the Daughter of the King. The King is thankful.

Conscious creativity combines essential elements conceived in solitude, silence, anger, joy, peace, love and grace. It also requires an audience. Dancing In The Rain is the actualization of peace in love when read, sometimes loud sometimes soft by you. In Anger, Silence, Solitude and Loneliness may enthusiastic joy be yours.

By Kurt Byron Huggins

"I let my anger shape my body

Until it was fierce"

ANGER

UNHAPPY TOGETHER 11

WHEN WORDS FAIL 13

ANGER...14

PROBLEM SOLVED 15

OIL AND WATER...16

TAKE EVERYTHING 17

I JUST DIDN'T KNOW..19

I CAN'T HELP YOU 21

WHEN ONE DOOR CLOSES..22

XY 24

EASIER SAID THAN DONE 25

THANK YOU...26

Unhappy Together

He: You've changed, you are not the woman
        I fell in love with
She: You are not the man I married
He: I know I promised to Love, honour and
        cherish but that is so painful right now
She: Maybe we should just go our separate way

He: What about the house?
She: the Kids?
He: the Cars?
She: the Family?
Both: What will our friends say?
        People just don't stay together anymore

        (Unspoken Words)
        He: It's cheaper to keep her
        She: It's better than starting over with
              some other loser!

He: My mother warned me about you
She: My father was right; I am too good for you!
He: I wish this was just a 5 year contract
        with the option to renew
        I would have been long gone

She: I can't stand you!
       I just wanted 2 kids with the same last
       name!

Both: Just stay out of my way and we'll meet
       in the middle for the kid's sake
He: Fine with me!
She: Go to hell... sperm donor!

When Words Fail

"Baby I'm sorry for everything" worked the first
and second time
But somewhere between 3 and 33
It lost its impact
And your words failed

"I love you more than life itself"
Used to make my toes curl
But somewhere between
"Go to Hell!" and "I don't care!"
The words "I love you" got lost
And they too failed

"I miss you, I miss you too"
Used to make me smile when you were away
Now they are just words that
No longer have the same meaning for me

The words are the same
They have not changed
It's the voice behind them that has failed
And the ears that hear that no longer
comprehends

Anger

Rage, vexation, fury, wrath
Hair of fire
Howling winds
Eyes that shoot ice and deadly darts
Voice of anguish
Shrieks of pain and death
Hands with deadly voltage
Feet of thunder that can shake the earth
I am enraged and no amount of profanity
Can soothe or quench my Anger
My Heart cries out "I am under attack!"
The hard shell forming around it starts breaking
My Heart is open and a flood of tears
cleanses my soul
And reconnects me to a power greater than self

Problem Solved

We spent a lot of time looking for balance
Trying to fix a deficit in our relationship
We tried supplementing
But that didn't work out
Someone was always left feeling short changed
There were far too many variables
The only solution was to remove something from
the equation
A simple answer
Why didn't I see this before?
If I remove you from my equation
Then we will both be equal

Oil And Water

We are both liquids
I can go where you can but we do not blend
One always remains on top of the other
We seem to connect only on the surface
Both having great qualities
Great properties
We are great for other industries
Great for other uses
But we are no good for each other
Something on the molecular level continues
to separate us
So let's admire our good qualities
And realize that we can never truly blend
We are great for others
but we are no good for each other

Take Everything

Take everything I have
It means nothing to me
Take everything I own
It has no value
Can't you see I have given you
The most important thing there is?
And that's my Heart

When I said "I love you"
I meant every word
They were magnified by every action
Every breath I took
I shared with you
Every meal I made for you was made with love
To nourish, to cherish, to share

Take everything I have
It means nothing to me
Take everything I own
It has no value
Can't you see I have given you the
Most important thing I own?
I have given you my Heart

If you have my Heart
You have the World
If you have my Heart
It comes fully packaged
Can't you see you've got me?

So you can take my House
Take all my belongings
Take everything I have;
They have no value to me
Can't you see I have given you
The most important thing I own?
And you had me long ago

I Just Didn't Know

You cried today and I just didn't know it
I was just too busy with the day to day of life
When you cried yesterday
I didn't know how to console you
So I gave you your space

Each time you cried I was overcome with guilt
Am I the cause of your tears?
I felt helpless and afraid
That if I couldn't console you, I'd lose you

I know what to do when our children cry
I hold them and tell them things will be alright
But when it comes to you
I just don't know what to do
If I held you would you turn me away?
Will things really be OK?
Only God can help me
Where is my book of instructions?

I come to you now with my Heart in hand
Please forgive me for all my wrongs
I didn't know
I just didn't know how to mend your Heart

I gave you your space
Now someone else has taken my place
Where did I go wrong?
What can I do to make you smile my way again?
I just don't want us to end
I didn't know
I just didn't know how to mend your broken Heart

I Can't Help You

I can't help you to get over me
It makes no sense
My feelings alone are so intense
I cannot bring a smile to your face
When my smile has been misplaced
The pain I feel, there is no medication for
It can only subside with the passing of time

All I can say is to seek the Sun
Its healing energy with help you'll grow
Take a breath
Take some time
Take a break
Get to know yourself
Just be
Cause I am trying to get over you
So please do not ask me to help you get over me

When One Door Closes

The door to my Heart is closing fast
Many have waited patiently outside the door
Yet few could enter
The security only allowed one VIP
For a long time he remained
He played with my Heart
Until one day he dropped it
And severe injury resulted
"Security" I screamed "Please remove this man
He is an imposter!"
How did we miss all that?
The results could have been fatal
I clung to my Heart in desperation
The pain was so intense
I fell to the floor and my security officer
Attempted to resuscitate
In spite of all his efforts
My Heart stopped that very day
In an instant my whole life flashed before my eyes
As I retraced my childhood
I came to the realization
That many of my dreams and goals
Remained unfulfilled
I relived the birth of my children
And marveled at the beauty of the experience.

There is some unfinished business here
I must return to this plane
Yet I am tempted by the option to leave
And go to a place filled with love and pure joy
"Wake up sweetHeart"
"Don't leave us; we need you"
"Please don't go"
Tear filled my eyes and I took a very big,
Very painful breath
Of the beginning of my new life.

XY

I was the X to your Y
And I believed it was written on our DNA
The story of our lives
Each chain a chapter
Every cell in tune with the other
Unspoken words
Messages understood
Somehow the electrical energy was changed
Signals no longer flowing freely
Free radical damage that cannot be repaired
Our communication has been compromised
Yet my vision is so clear
I see you now for what you are
You are not just my EX
You are my Why?!

Easier Said than Done

I tried everything to get away from you
I tried subtracting you from me
I cried
I prayed
But you refused to go

You are mine you say
I belong to no one is my reply
Still I can't stop thinking of you
I guess it's easier said than done
Easy for me to say but we are far from done

We have a history
Good or bad it's ours
We have children
Ours to care for
Try as I may you will always be
Part of this unsolvable equation

The answer appears to be 3
Depending on the variables
The solution could be more
Are you part of it?
Yes you are a factor of one that remains

Thank You

If loving me the way you do is the very best
you can do
How can I stay angry with you?
I can honor the time spent
The tender moments and the lessons learnt

Thank you for the laughter and the tears
Thank you for the many years
My life has been blessed by you
Even though my path continues away from you
I will always have love and respect for you

Continue to grow
Continue to love
Continue to be who you are meant to be
Remember me with fond memories
I love you my friend

*"My silence gave me an opportunity
to get to know myself"*

SILENCE

DAUGHTER OF THE KING...31

IS THERE SOMEONE ELSE? 33

MUSIC..35

VULNERABLE 37

FRAGILE 38

THE BEST GIFT 39

CHILDHOOD FRIEND 41

PLEASE DON'T GO...43

BUTTERFLY 45

CHILD OF THE UNIVERSE...47

DO YOU KNOW ME? 49

MY GIRL...50

THE HEAT OF AUGUST..51

IT'S JUST SEX...52

Marcia A. Williams

Daughter Of The King

Can I be so bold to say
The Universe understands and feels my emotions?
When I am troubled the clouds come
When I cry it rains
Could I be so special?
Yes, I am the Daughter of the King

When I fight with my conscience
I feel a storm brewing
When I reach a new level of consciousness,
The skies clear
When I smile, the Sun shines
Could I be so special?
Yes I can
I am the Daughter of the King

When there is a song in my heart
I hear the birds sing its refrain
How do they know?
I know why they sing for me
I am the Daughter of the King

My father has blessed me with the gift of song
I want to honor him and make him so proud
When I walk into a room
It becomes quiet and calm
As if everyone is waiting for me to speak

What will I say?
I will tell them my Father sends his love
And their souls will be healed
Who am I?
I am the Daughter of the King

Marcia A. Williams

Is There Someone Else?

Funny - you left me for SOMEONE else.
You thought I had SOMEONE else.
You broke my heart for SOMEONE else.
"Is SOMEONE else more important then me?" you ask
"More important than your family?"
I don't understand you I said
There has always been SOMETHING else -
SOMETHING that fulfills me like no one can
Don't be jealous, you've always known.

When you asked me to choose
I chose SOMETHING
I chose MUSIC
You looked confused
The late nights
The telephone calls
The elation
Oh! You thought it was another?
You are mistaken
By the way it's too bad you left me for SOMEONE else

I met SOMEONE else who promised to love me
Unconditionally
Yesterday I was asked the very same question
"Is there SOMEONE else?"
Yes there will always be SOMETHING else
There will always be my first love
There will always be ... MUSIC

Music

I fell in love with Music
It took all that I had
And demanded so much of those around me
They could not understand my commitment
Music became my master and I dedicated my soul
To become a messenger of Love

The man I loved felt jealous
Of that which he could not see or understand
Life for him was empty and lonely
Music was my Master
And I gladly became its Slave
No distance was too far to travel for that which I love
Music became my man, my lover, my only friend
And when all was gone
All that remained was a sad refrain

I sang it with such feeling that it sent shivers
Through its listeners
They could understand the feelings of desire, of
Longing of wanting
But only one who has sacrificed as much as I
Could appreciate the meaning and the level of
Commitment required

Music became my Master
And gladly I became its Slave
No distance was too far to travel
I was there for the long ride
Willingly accepted my role
Everyone around me was silenced
And all that remained was a voice crying out
Fighting for a melody

I refused to be silenced
I have something to say, you will listen
Truth, my truth will be told
Everything I have
My very breath is what was demanded
So here I stand alone with nothing to give
But a melody I sacrificed everything for

Vulnerable

*(Adj. Susceptible, weak, defenseless, helpless,
at risk, in a weak position)*

Please define that word for me
Is it a state of mind?
Does it imply a certain amount of innocence?
Can it be taken advantage of?
If the person who is described as vulnerable
Can reduce their attackers to pity or compassion
Who is then vulnerable?

Fragile

The human body has over 3000 parts moving
together
That takes us from here to there
All of our bones can be broken and fixed
Healed at any time
But I can guarantee you that nothing
No fracture hurts more than a broken heart...

My broken heart reduced my strong stature to the
fetal position
And sent my tear ducts into overdrive
Breathing became the most difficult and
important task of every day

The medical community can operate and mend
every fracture
They can add plates and pins
But they cannot mend a broken heart
At times this fracture can be fatal
Others can take years to heal

Marcia A. Williams

The Best Gift

I had the perfect gift for you
The ideal gift for any occasion
You would have loved it
I did not see you for a very long time so
I carried it with me everywhere I went
Just in case I ran into you
I tried my best to keep it safe
Precious cargo I warned anyone
who tried to come near it
It does not belong to you
Please do not touch it
I heard you were coming to town
I was delighted
Finally I could give my gift to you
On the way to you I got distracted
Tired from carrying your present for so long
I enlisted the help of another
Just hold it for a moment I asked
When he saw the gift he became jealous
Something this precious should be mine he said
No please give it back,
It belongs to a dear friend I told him

Oops he said as it slipped thru his fingers
He broke the most precious gift I had for you
my dear friend
That gift was my Heart
You would have loved it too
When it's open it loves deeply
All I have for you now are the pieces I've picked up
Parts of it shattered never to be put together again
All I have for you now are the pieces I could find

Marcia A. Williams

Childhood Friend

Childhood friend its time to say goodbye
We have shared and given so much
To fun and games
The time has come to grow and change
Do I love you any less?
Oh no my playmate
But its time to grow up

I reminisce of all the times we shared in the park
Rolling down the hills like Jack and Jill
Oh what fun we had!
I didn't want anyone to get hurt
We were carefree and
The World was our playground

The sands of time moved rapidly
We ran away and left our toys
Hoping we could go back and reclaim them
There is no going back
We have to face an uncertain future

Wow, look how much you've grown!
No! It's me; I've grown
You just got bigger
But you are still the same carefree one
That I loved in my youth

I am not that little one anymore
Time has tempered my playfulness
I am fierce, I am becoming ME
I know its frightening for you
But I have a message for the World
And I can't get there holding on to you
I have to continue to grow and I need my space
Don't be hurt my friend
You may never understand my calling
But the World needs me and I must go
You may follow if you wish but I cannot carry you
I am not walking away from you my friend
I am walking towards the future

Marcia A. Williams

Please Don't Go

My childhood friend I love you more than life itself
We have so much fun when we play together!
We can watch movies or rent some video games
We can play for hours
Aren't you having fun?
Let's go to the park and play like we used to

Where are you going?
I thought you were having fun too
Why are you leaving me?
Aren't you afraid of the big cruel world out there?
Who will protect you?
What if someone hurts you?
You can always come back and play
I will always take you back

Did you find another friend?
Are they better than me?
Do they have nicer toys?
If they don't have nicer toys, why are you going?

What's that you say you have
Response...Responsibility?
What it that? Is it a new game?
Can I play too?
I don't have any other friends
How will I manage without you?
Please don't go!

Butterfly

I fell in love with a beautiful Butterfly
I loved her so much
Her wings were so beautiful
And when she danced...It was a sight to behold

I wanted to keep her for myself
So I got the best jar I could find
Placed her in it
I punched several holes in the lid of the best jar
So she would have plenty of air
I would cherish her everyday!
What a prize!
I showed her to some of my friends
And they too marveled at
The beautiful creature I had found

One day a man came and said
"Can't you see her wings are damaged?"
"You're wrong! I protected her and loved her

I fed her the best food I could find"
"She's ok", I said
"You must set her free!" he said
"You are destroying this beautiful creature.
 You are meant to share her with the world.
A thing of beauty should not be bottled up;
It should be shared"

I looked at my Butterfly and finally realized
That I was selfish and I was killing
This beautiful creature
I had captured not so long ago
So I opened the jar
And with a full Heart I set her free
She flew high into the heavens
I hope she will be happy
And maybe one day she will bless me
With her beauty again

Marcia A. Williams

Child of the Universe

I am a traveler on the road of life
I have no map yet I travel in safety
I am a Child of the Universe
Born to make changes

I have met many down this road
Strangers to friends to my enemies
They too are a blessing for they will challenge you
And reveal your true nature
With my open Heart as my guide
I am a Child of the Universe
Born to make changes

I will touch you with loving hands heal you
Soothe you with my voice
Grace you with my presence
Bless you with my spirit
I am a Child of the Universe
Born to make changes

The road blocks on this road
Is merely a test of my faith
The purpose they serve is
To strengthen my conviction
And empower me for the road ahead
The road signs are people who serve as guides
They answer my questions
Offer support, a place to rest
And directions for the next part of my journey
I am a Child of the Universe
Born to make changes

The journey continues on...
I am a Child of the Universe
Destined to make changes

Do You Know Me?

Do you know me?
I've never met you before
How can you say you know me?
When I am just getting to know myself

I am redefining self
I am "blossoming" my friends say
Welcome back my brothers say
Where have you been?
We've really missed you

I realize I've been gone for quite some time
But I'm back
And yes I am someone you will want to know

My Girl

My Girl has style
She has more than presence
she has circumference
When she steps outside the whole World knows
she has arrived
The trees move their leaves to have a peek
And Squirrels drop their nuts to applause
Her clothing hugs her body as if that is where
they desire to be
Her hair shines like a crown that graces the head
of a true Queen
The Sun is her spotlight and the wind
kisses her face
The only thing in competition with My Girl
is the Sun
Her smile can dazzle and melt any heart
Any man would love to be at her side
And yet she has chosen me to be her one and
only choice
My Woman, My Queen, My Girl

Marcia A. Williams

The Heat Of August

When desire creeps up and down my spine
A strange energy takes over my body
becomes magnetic
Every inch of me becomes desirable
Each strand of my hair, my eyes, my hands, my lips
The small of my back sends out a distinct call that
can be heard
They come from miles around
Even the shaking of my locks leaves them aroused
They are puzzled by their uncontrollable desire and
I am reminded of the ancient lure of a Woman
I am on top of the World and the World
would be mine
in exchange for my charms
Riches I have; what I want from you is much more
primal in nature
Come to me I beckon and they kneel at my feet
Begging to indulge in the sweet nectar that can
only be found in my paradise
Satisfaction is just a touch away
Right here
Right now
Come to me and live!

It's Just Sex

You asked me for a piece of me
"It's just Sex"
Part of me that I hold in high regard
"It's just Sex"
Something that I share only with the man I love
"It's just Sex"
For you it's just Sex
For me it's so much more
"It's just Sex!"
Maybe it's just your Sex that places such little
value
On the gift of myself
So if it's just sex
You can have just that
With someone else

"My solitude created beautiful reflections"

SOLITUDE

BECOMING...57

IN A MOMENT 57

SILENCE IS 60

CHILDREN OF LIGHT..62

MY LITTLE ISLAND 64

THE CIRCLE OF THE ELDERS 65

GOD STILL SPEAKS 66

LETTING GO 67

MARETA...68

ANTICIPATION OF TOUCH 70

I AM BEING LEAD 71

WHEN I AM IN MY VALLEY 72

THE DANCE 74

I NEED SOMEONE 75

IN TIME...75

WHY...76

Becoming

I let my anger shape my body
Until it was fierce
My silence gave me an opportunity
to get to know myself
My solitude created beautiful reflections
Loneliness gave me an environment
in which to be creative
And to build lasting friendships

In a Moment

"May all our loved ones live on
in all of God's creations!"

When my time on Earth ended
I asked for one last wish
Anything was the answer
How long do I have?
A reason, four seasons, a year
That's marvelous

I've always wanted to be a cloud
In a wink I was a cloud
Soft and fluffy
I made some designs that children pointed at
I played guess what shapes with them

I then became a rainbow
Beautiful and colorful
A symbol of hope
Stretching across the skies after a rainfall

I became the sunbeams that warmed the Earth
Then grains of sand in a vast desert
A drop of water in the deep blue sea
I rode on the back of a giant Whale
And swam with the Dolphins off the coast

I danced with the Wolves in the northern forest
And howled at a full Moon
I became part of the Northern Lights
I saw beauty and there was music
in and around me
It was amazing

I've always wanted to be a Diamond
But not too fast
A lump of coal for a moment then a Diamond in
all its brilliance
I became lava hot inside the Earth's core
To a Seagull flying along the shores
So many wonders to behold
Four seasons I was told

I wanted to experience what its like to be
Hot . . . cold
Light . . . dark
Wind . . . rain
Hard . . . soft
The tallest Mountain
The smallest pebble
The smallest bud
To the tallest tree

For a moment
I experienced everything I could ever dream of
I could be in or be part of all of God's creation
And finally realized the words to my favorite hymn
"How Great Thou Art"

Silence Is

Silence is not golden
Where laughter once resides
Silence now exists
The quiet is haunting
And a painful reminder of what is missing
Where children once played...Silence remains
Again to remind us that the children have grown
Where toys and handprints once decorated
A busy house
Silence lives

Not all Silence is golden
Some are painful reminders of what is missing
Joy, laughter, friends, family and love
Silence is here to teach me something important

Its here to remind me of the things I should value
Don't value the Stereo
Value the music that resonated from it
That soothe the soul

Don't value the Television
Value the time spent in front of it
With your family
Watching your favorite shows
Value fun times and laughter
Don't place value on a House
Value the things that made it a home and
The warmth that remained inside its doors

Silence... you are a great Teacher
At the moment I am silent and my pen speaks
And I have learnt so much

Children of Light

You have been chosen to deliver
A message to the World
A world so unaware
So full of Anger, Hate, Indifference
You are blessed and highly favored
You are the Children of Light

Others say you are too sensitive
As if sensitivity is a crime
It's time for sensitive to take its place
To love, to heal, to renew
Children of Light
You come out of darkness
How can this be?
The darkness empowers you
It tries to consume you
But you rise above it
With the help of your guides and the Creator
You shine for the World to see

You are blessed and highly favored
Your are God's gift to a dying world
Your love can heal it
And yes your tears can make its rivers and streams
whole again

We can all do our part
From every corner of the globe
For the Children of Light
Are more powerful than you think
Our ancestors are on your side
The spirits of the air, soil and all of its elements
Are your allies

You are blessed and highly favored
Chosen to heal a world that is dying
Let your hands heal the trees, the soil,
The barrier that surrounds our planet
Let your heart be your guide
Let us renew our connections with every atom
Everyone
We are all One

Children of Like, Children of Light
You shine in the darkness
To save a World that is healing
A World that is healing because of your love.

My Little Island

On the days when the world gets too loud
I retreat to my little island
Where my helpers greet me with my favorite drink
and my slippers
I can unwind
Wash my cares away in the peaceful waters
That surrounds my place of serenity

When I've wash my cares of the day away
I retreat to my easy chair
Where I can be soothe by sweet music in front of
a roaring fire
The warmth provides yet another level
of satisfaction
And the smile returns to my face
Just in time for the sun to set in the horizon
"Thank you I will take it from here..."

The Circle of the Elders

"We know why we have been called here. It is time to summon the powers of the elements. The future scream cries of destruction and we are running out of time. Is everyone here? We all have a role to play and it will take everything we have. Some of us will not make it. Are you willing to make that sacrifice for the future of mankind?"

The loud whisper "Yes" filled our sacred halls as the ceremony for the healing of the Planet began. I was afraid but I knew it had to be done and the responsibility we had to the future.

A great blast of light sent some of our Brothers and Sisters across the globe, others were left not remembering what had just taken place.

We had saved our Planet but in doing so got separated; how will we find each other?

God Still Speaks

God still speaks to his people
Can you hear his voice?
He tells us to love one another as he has loved us
Do you hear his voice?
He says keep my Commandments
Do you know them?
He says love your Neighbors
Do you know what that means?
A simple act of kindness goes a long way everyday

Everything on this plane of existence is merely
A test of our faith
A lesson in love
Your coin to life everlasting
How many you collect on this journey is up to you...

When God calls me home
I want to have collected enough love
To fill my Heart
Enough for many lifetimes
Let my ears be open to hear God's voice
Let my eyes be open to see goodness in others
Let my hands do your works
Let my voice be a blessing to others
Let it bring peace and encouragement in their lives
I am your humble servant

Letting Go

I wanted someone else to lean on
I needed something strong to hold on to
I was like a ship in a storm
I could neither see nor steer my course

I found myself in an ocean of tears
Even when the storm had subsided I was lost
My sails were damaged
And I could not find my way back to sure

"Miss, are you lost; why are you so sad?
Can I help you?"
"Yes" I thought finally someone to hold on to
I was mistaken
It was just a rescue
And my Rescuer had no intention
Of staying with me
He had done his duty

"Please do not leave me here alone," I pleaded
"This is unfamiliar soil; how will I manage?"
His reply was, "You are a strong woman
Everyday forever"
"Thank you Princess I have been blessed by you"
He took his leave of me
My life was changed forever

MARETA

"I'm Grandma's favorite," No I am!...
Grandma who is your favorite?!!"

My Grandmother's love is unconditional
She sprinkled all of us with it and we're blessed
Strong and Firm she guided us
With love and discipline.

Mother of my Father, you have blessed me with
Your Heart,
Your smile and your silver hair
Everyone that looks upon me knows that
I am a product of your unconditional love.

You watched me grow
You taught me how to pray
You made me feel so special
Like every smile that came my way
Had a heaping spoonful of your love

When I was overcome with sickness
Many thought I would not make it
You washed and surrounded me
With loving arms you brought me safely
Back home

Story time on rainy days
Loving hands that combed my hair
An Angel you must have been
My Heart cried for you when God convinced you
To come back home
I see your smile in the clouds
And I know that you have and always will be
A great love of my life

Anticipation of Touch

Anticipation of your touch
Butterflies take flight
What an amazing feeling
Can I bottle it up and share it with the World?

Intensity, heat, Heart racing
The body responds favorably
Fingers, lips quiver, toes curl
What an amazing feeling
I'd love to share it with the World

This is love
The bliss of love requires no additives
It is self sustaining
Requires only two to take it to the next level
The first step takes place in the mind

Marcia A. Williams

I Am Being Lead

I am climbing up a very steep hill
I am almost at the top
I am astonished by progress
How did I get here?
Am I being lead?

I become afraid
I start slipping downhill
I am being Lead
Feet, hands, tired from all the work

I am in a bad situation
I know the proper course of action
Yet I fail to move
I am being Lead

Finally my hand is forced
I'm being led to a better place I am told
I am being lead with some painful hesitation
I am being lead

When I Am In My Valley

What do I do when enough is enough?
When I have reached the end of my ropes
And everything around me leaves me unfulfilled?

Where do I go when every door closes?
I look up
There is only one way out
It's upwards and onwards
The only way is up

What do I do when my Heart aches
And longs for a familiar beat?
Where it was secure and restful
Where do I turn?
What do I do when my Heart breaks right at home?

I resist an overwhelming urge to retreat within
I fight with thoughts of defeat
I pray for guidance
And I look up
There is only one way out
It's upwards and onwards

Marcia A. Williams

On the days when I am in my valley
I am reminded that I am not alone
Help comes in many forms
A ray of sunshine
A bird singing sweetly
A smile from a stranger
The voice of a friend

On the days when I am in my valley
I look up and I am reminded
That even though I may feel lonely
I am never alone
And I am grateful for my faith

The Dance

The Weatherman called for rain today
All day
How will I manage?
Last year it rained a lot
Every time it rained I was crying
I started to believe that I was the cause
I cried for myself
I cried for my friends
I cried for everyone I had lost
I cried for the entire planet
Today I decided to dance
I looked in my archives of music
I danced to Reggae, Soca and Calypso
I did the Cha Cha
The Salsa and the Meringue
I even did the slow graceful dance of the Swans
When it was freestyle time
The rain poured with such intensity
I danced even more
It rained until I was exhausted
I told my friend later that evening
She said, "Describe your freestyle dancing"
I described my movements in great detail
She laughed and said
"Congratulations my love,
You were doing a Rain dance!"

I Need Someone

I need someone to fight for me
Someone who would die for me
To stand up and speak out
On my behalf
To look out for my best interest
To walk through the fires of Hell
To win great battles for me
To love me unconditionally
To be my best friend
Of all the things I need
And desire the most
I need that someone to be ME

In Time

In time all the things I worried about
Will be a distant memory
In time many of my goals will be accomplished
Others well within my reach
In time all the friends that once hurt me
In retrospect would have taught me
valuable life lessons
In time I will grow into the one I am meant to be
Someone I can be proud of
In time I will publicly give light to all of my flaws
And I will call them human

WHY

Why does my heart feel safe in your company?
Why is it not stressed or strained?
Why is it steady and strong?
Why do you utter words of sweet contentment?
Why does my heart long for a home?

I am not worthy of your devotion
I am flawed and unsure
There are others more deserving of your
love and affection
What can I offer you?
I have nothing

I could not possibly be what you've been looking for
I have been hiding for so long
I thought I could just slip by unnoticed
Why are you looking my way?

Please reconsider
You must be mistaken
I am not worthy of your devotion
Please love someone else

"Loneliness gave me an environment
in which to be creative
And to build lasting friendships"

LONELINESS

I FOUND A FRIEND 81

THE REASON WHY I SMILE 82

UNDERSTANDING 83

MY MOTHER 84

BABY 86

DADDY SAID 87

BITTER SWEET...88

NEW BEGINNING 90

NEW LOVE 91

CHAIN REACTION..92

CHAIN REACTION II 93

TURN OVER ANEW.. 95

GOD IS WITH ME..96

I Found a Friend

I cried so much the tears left me
I cried so hard the sound disappeared
I fell tired and distraught
And wondered if I would ever feel whole again

Until I realized I am whole
God made me in His image
Brilliant and whole
Soon I met someone who offered friendship
We laughed and talked for hours about nothing
and everything
And it was then I realized
I have found a friend

The Reason Why I Smile

Yesterday I didn't know your name
Today you are the reason why I smile
The miles between us diminishes as your laughter
echoes in my ear
My smile is loud you say
I say my smile is yours and you are
the reason why I smile
Life has such wonderful surprises in store for me
You are one of them then
And I look forward to my future
with great expectations

The things you say are so precious yet it is
the sound of your voice
That has captured my Heart
My Heart is no stranger to love
It has felt great joy and the pain that comes from
the loss of love

Today my Heart is steady and at peace
It does not flutter
It anticipates
It smiles and knows the reason why
Beautiful, wonderful, amazing, captivating,
funny you
You are the reason why I smile

Understanding

Understanding is all I can offer you
I can offer you love
But understanding how you define love
Is the first thing I need to do

What language do you speak
when you speak of love?
Is your language universal?
Does it contain symbols?
Is it easy to translate?
Is it easy to understand?

What happens if I make an error
or say the wrong thing?
Will I have your understanding?
Since understanding is all I can offer you
Will that translate to your understanding of me?

My Mother

Mom I just didn't know
How much you love me
The words were not said often
But Oh now I understand

When you carried me safely inside you
You were loving me
When my little hands and feet moved
And you smiled and rubbed your belly
You loved me

When you brought me safely into the World
And when our eyes met for the first time
That love was amplified
From that day onward
We had an unwritten contract
Of Unconditional Love

When you held me
When you fed me
When you washed and clothed me
When you kissed me
You loved me

All the things you do and continue to do
Says love through and through
There are few words that can express
My infinite gratitude
For everything you've done for me

Mother, Teacher, Mentor, lifelong Friend
My words are just ten percent of the love
I have for you
Thank you from the bottom of my Heart
Thank you for being so loving

Baby

Flesh of my flesh
Skin of my skin
Child born of love
Carefully constructed
With the building blocks of my Ancestors
From Heaven to Earth
To teach
To love
To join me on my journey
I promise to give you the very best of me
The best way I can
Welcome to my World
My precious little one

Daddy Said

Daddy said, "Stay close baby, don't stray too far"
Daddy says "play safe and stay close to your Mom"
"What a big girl; you are growing up too fast"
Daddy said, "who is this boy and who is he to you?"
"Dad I am a big girl now and I'm going off to
University"
"Yes this boy is my Fiancée and we are getting
married"
Daddy said, "Don't put all your eggs in one basket"
"Daddy…Yes I'm sure"
Daddy said, "You don't have to do this you know"
"Daddy…Yes I'm sure"
Daddy said, "where are my grandchildren?"
"Here is your grandson Daddy"
"Are you ok my baby? You don't look well"
"Don't worry you don't have to have another one,
Daddy is happy with this one"
Daddy said, "Your Mom and I miss you very much"
"I know Daddy I will try to come around more"
"Daddy here is your other grandson"
"He is very handsome, but how are you?"
"Daddy I'm fine"
"Daddy I'm not so happy, is love really enough?"
"I love him Daddy but I'm not very happy
And I miss my family"

Bitter Sweet

Why? Why? Why?
I have asked so many times
Is my life so Bitter Sweet
The answer is all around me
And it's not just me
Many others have felt the same
And have asked the very same question
Why is life so Bitter Sweet?
Why do we win the war and I lose my comrades?
Why when my Album hits number 1
Did I lose my Mother?
Why do I find the greatest love of my life
And lose them to terminal illness?
Why do I love so much and get nothing in return?
Why? Why? Why?
Why am I so physically strong and emotionally
vulnerable?
Why is the person of my dreams
Married to someone else?

The answer is balance...
We don't want the Sunshine without the Rain
We can't have East without West
We don't want to be down without the chance
To get back up
The answer is great

Good and Bad
We need both for balance
Yes you lost your comrades but they gave their lives
for victory and freedom
Yes you lost your Mother but she gave you life
Yes you lost the greatest love of your life
But you found and experienced great love
When you love; love without expectations
Your emotional strength will improve
The person of your dreams
Should be married to you
Life is balance
Life is hard and soft
It is what it is...
Bitter Sweet is life in its balance

New Beginning

Sadness is like a barren wasteland
where nothing grows
There is rain with the occasional
ray of sunshine
I wept bitterly through the rainy season
Finally new life sprouted
And soon a garden green with lush vegetation
A new blossom sprouted
The beginning of beauty and colors so vibrant
it filled my senses
I am awakened to
the new sweet smell of happiness

New Love

I told myself that if I had to stand with someone
Who does not have my back
I would rather stand alone
I told my heart that it cannot be trusted to make
sound decisions
Now here you are to test my will
To shake my foundation
Why are you here?
I am not the one for you
I am a flight risk
I am afraid
So afraid
But
I would be willing to try again...
With you

Chain Reaction

With a thought
Your scent enters my office
How strange
Where are you?
Are you thinking of me?
I take a deep breath
A warm feeling comes over me
A smile dawns inside my soul
I pick up the phone to make another connection
Hi there
What you doing?
A smile
A sinful thought
I can feel you in my riches
My temperature rises
I lower my head
I feel the urge to cross my legs
Squeeze the cushion of my chair
I am thirsty
I bite my bottom lip
Another deep breath
I slowly loosen the button of my blouse
I exhale
What are you doing to me?
I can't do this here
My co-workers will talk
Damn this feels nice!
Can we finish this off at home?

Chain Reaction II

The work day is finally over
Can't wait to get home
Anxious for what the evening has to offer
Action or Romance I wonder
Still connected
I imagine a clear path
Cars start moving out of the way
As if they know my purpose
I smile as the path to you is cleared
The back of my neck tingles
I reach up to rub it
My vitals are elevated in anticipation
I exhale
Let my hair down
My locks fall to my shoulder
I shake them
Run my finger through them
The man in the car next to me sees me
He smiles as if he too knows what's in store
An essential breath
My hand reaches down to rub my thighs
Hoping to hold back this brimming dam of desire
Almost there
I can taste you on my lips
I shift in my seat
I exhale

I pull into the driveway
The snow on my car has melted away
I grab my purse
I bolt for the door
He waits for me
I am ready
Forget the Romance for now baby
Round one should be action
I wrap my legs around him
He welcomes me in and closes the front door

Turn Over Anew

I want to write a new story…a love story
One that will go down in the history books of stories
One of great love and respect
Where wants, needs and desires are met
Where smiles are abundant, joy is commonplace
yet never taken for granted
Where the words "I love you" means the gift of oneself
Where actions are coupled with
tenderness and meaning
When coming home is anticipated with butterflies
and great expectations
Where home is truly where the Heart is
and will remain
The family's motto will be
"If God is for us who can be against us?"
And it will be my story

God Is With Me

I am not alone
God is with me
I am loved and protected
God is with me
In my darkest hour
God is with me
In my moments of great joy
God is with me
When my friends forsake me
God is with me
When I make a new friend
God is with me
Through every blessed moment of my life
I give thanks
For I know that God is with me

Marcia A. Williams is a singer, poet and writer. Her pen and her voice are her instruments of artistic expression. In song, Marcia's "velvet smooth" voice will warm your heart. Her spoken word poems are captivating. Her literary work is powerful, filled with insights — at times personal — but always universal. In short they're about expressions of love, faith and hope.

Marcia is a graduate of York University where she completed a Bachelor of Arts in English.
Writing however was not a gift this talented vocalist thought she possessed. Her writing began as an act of survival, an outlet for creativity, clarity of thought and self discovery.

Her journey has taken her from helping other artists shine, providing supporting vocals to stepping out to centre stage where she has quickly won over fans with her poetry.
This book is the beginning of Marcia's journey toward becoming the passionate and acclaimed writer she unknowingly has been preparing for all her life.

CPSIA information can be obtained at www.ICGtesting.com
Printed in the USA
BVOW031322290712

296427BV00001B/3/P